Gerngross · Puchta · Becker
PLAYWAY 4

PUPIL'S BOOK

W0189255

1 Let's go shopping

⭐ **1** Work in pairs. Can you remember the missing numbers? Take notes.

ten	?	?	?	fourteen	?	sixteen
seventeen	?	?	twenty	twenty-one	?	?
twenty-four	?	?	?	twenty-eight	twenty-nine	?

⭐ **2** 🔊 1 Listen and point. In pairs, point and say.

10	ten
20	twenty
30	thirty
40	forty
50	fifty
60	sixty
70	seventy
80	eighty
90	ninety
100	a hundred
200	two hundred
300	three hundred

SHOE SHOP

£ 100 £ 40 £ 90 £ 60 £ 300 £ 20 £ 10 £ 30 £ 50 £ 80 £ 70 £ 200

⭐ **3** Play the memory game.

How much are the green shoes?

They're …

📷 Poster 1   AB S. 2

★ 4 1 3–4 Listen. Sing the song.

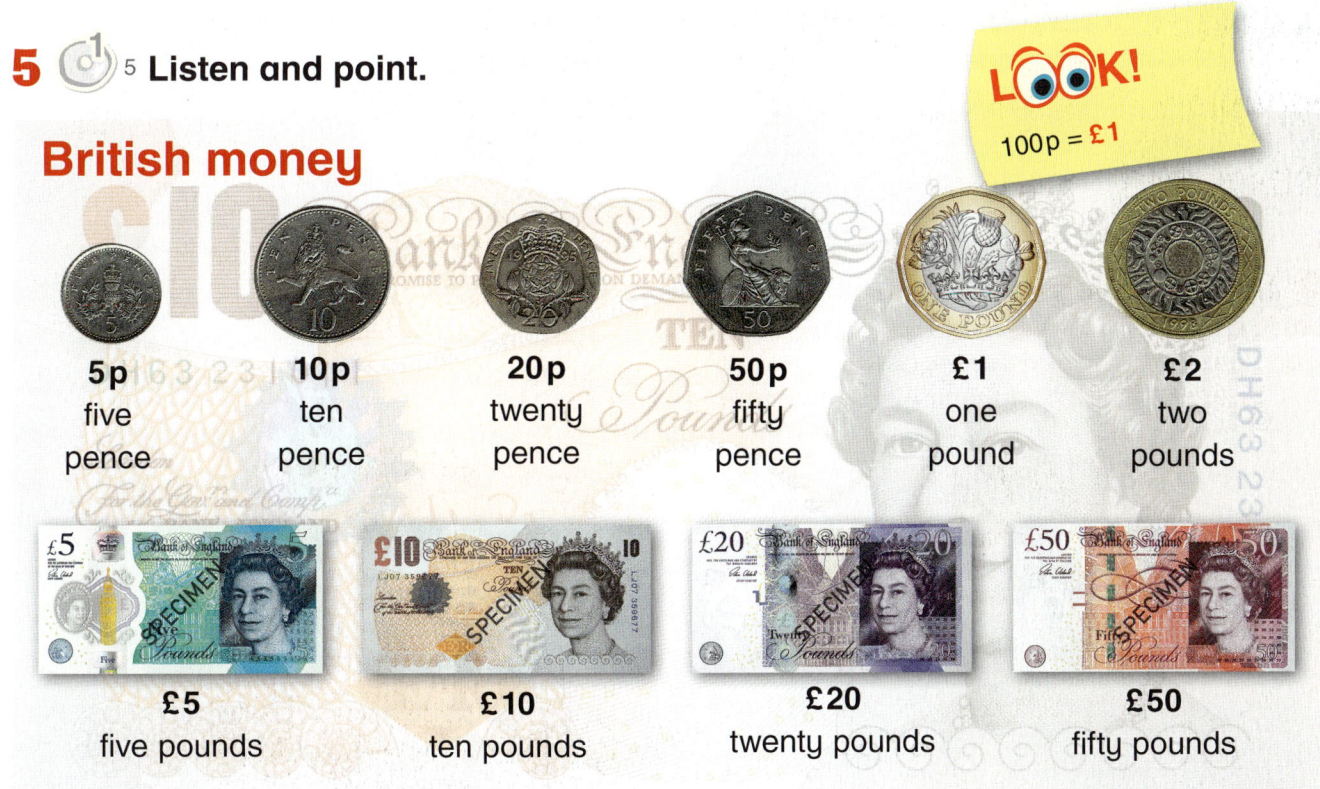

A hundred big black ravens

Ninety …

Seventy …

Fifty …

Thirty …

Ten …

A hundred big black ravens
are flying after you.
They want to steal your piggy bank.
So this is what you do:

You pull a face,
you shake your fist,
you shout, 'No way!'
and ten fly away.

Eighty …

Sixty …

Forty …

Twenty …

★ 5 1 5 Listen and point.

LOOK!
100p = £1

British money

5p
five
pence

10p
ten
pence

20p
twenty
pence

50p
fifty
pence

£1
one
pound

£2
two
pounds

£5
five pounds

£10
ten pounds

£20
twenty pounds

£50
fifty pounds

KV 1   AB S. 3   3

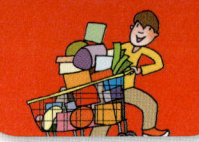

1 Let's go shopping

6 Listen and point.

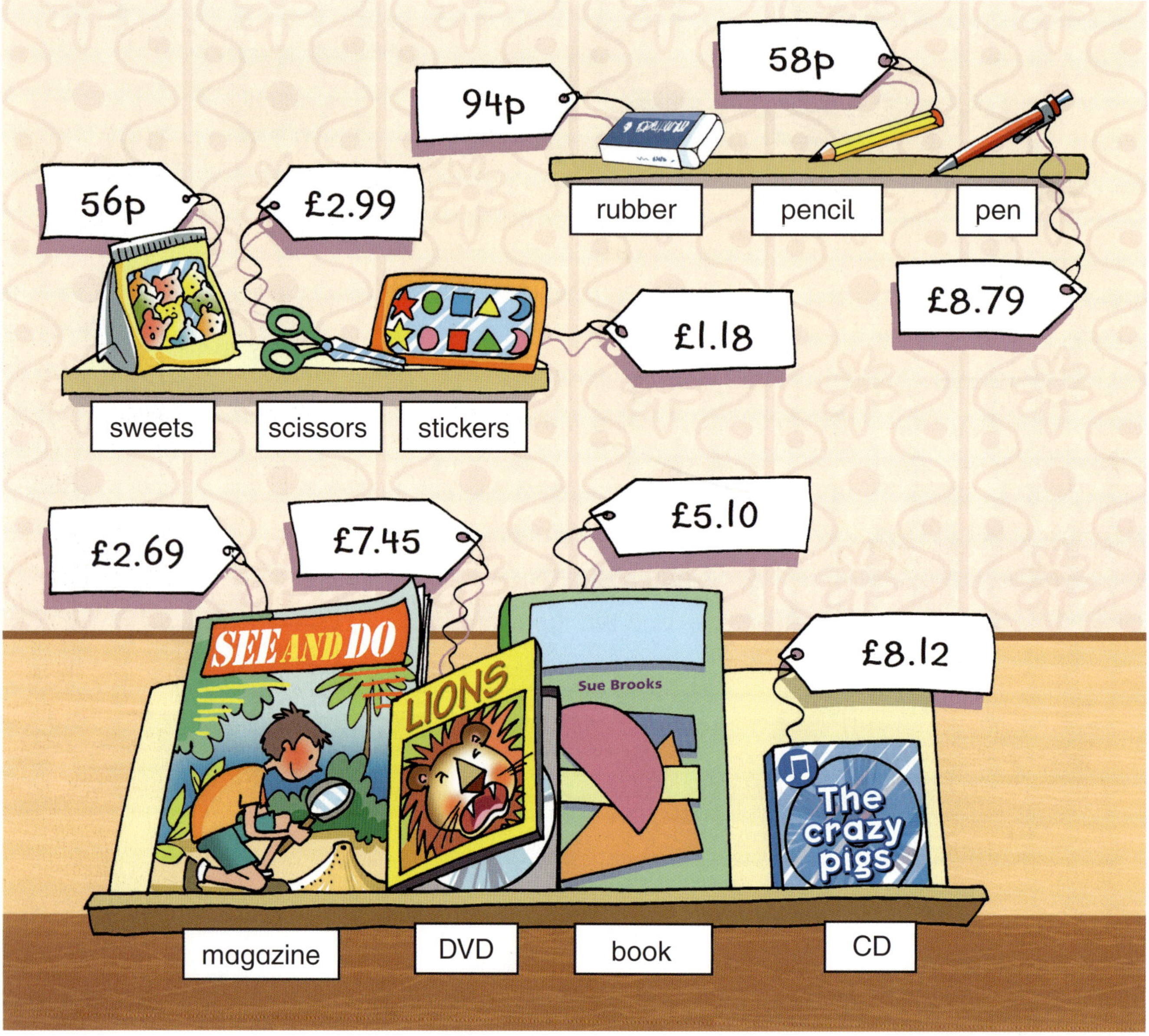
94p
58p
56p
£2.99
rubber
pencil
pen
£8.79
£1.18
sweets
scissors
stickers
£2.69
£7.45
£5.10
£8.12
SEE AND DO
LIONS
Sue Brooks
The crazy pigs
magazine
DVD
book
CD

7 Look at number 6. Ask and answer.

LOOK!

How much **is** the book? – It'**s** …

How much **are** the sweet**s**? – They'**re** …

How much is the magazine?
It's …

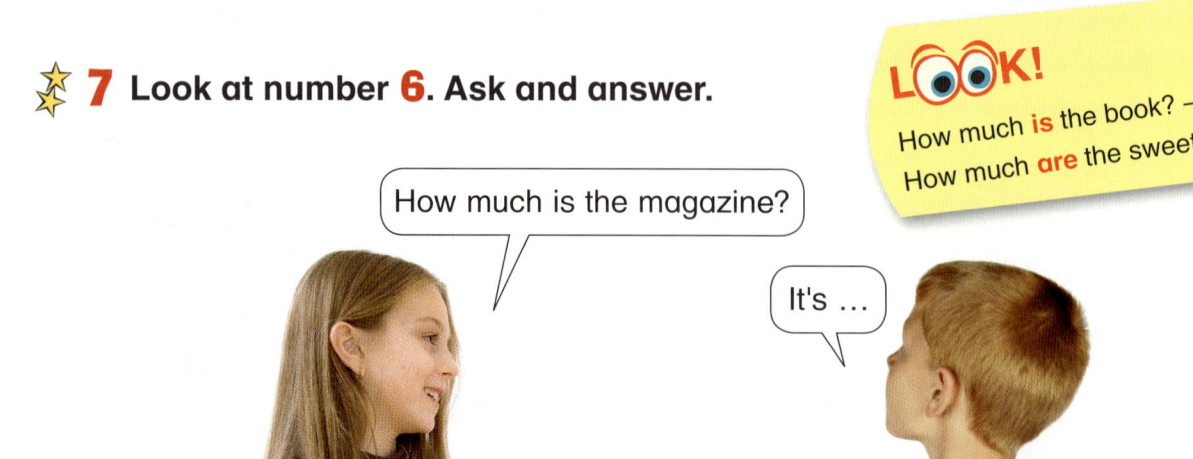

Going shopping

⭐ **8** **Watch the story and say words you remember. Finish the sentences.**

1
There's no food in the house.

Can … ?

2
Let's …

I haven't got a pen.

3
OK, I'm ready. Let's go.

Sorry, Dad. …

4
It's nice, isn't it?

It's …

⭐ **9**   11 **Listen and read.**

Oscar:	Dad, there's no food in the house.
Clara:	Can you go shopping?
Dad:	Sorry, I'm busy.
Oscar:	Please, Dad.
Dad:	OK. Let's make a shopping list.
Oscar:	Cheese, eggs and milk.
Clara:	Apples, carrots and oranges.
Dad:	OK. Are you coming with me?
Oscar & Clara:	Sorry, Dad. We're going to the park.

⭐ **10 Do a role play.**

⭐ **11** 💿 12 **Listen and read.**

Stella:	Excuse me, can you help me, please?
Shop assistant:	Yes, of course.
Stella:	I'd like a red T-shirt.
Shop assistant:	OK, come with me.
Leo:	This T-shirt is nice.
Stella:	Yeah, I like it too. How much is it?
Shop assistant:	It's £8.99.
Leo:	Stella, these trainers are cool.
Stella:	Wow, they look great.
Leo:	How much are they?

Shop assistant:	They're £125.
Stella:	OK, I'll take the T-shirt.
Shop assistant:	Anything else?
Stella:	No, thanks. That's all.
Shop assistant:	£8.99, please.
Stella:	Here you are.
Leo and Stella:	Goodbye.
Shop assistant:	Bye.

⭐ **12 Change the dialogue in 11 and act it out.**

My text ✏️

⭐ **13 Read. Write your own text.**

My text

I often go shopping with my mum. The supermarket is in White Street. There we buy bread, milk, vegetables, eggs and cheese.

⭐ **14 Read. Write your own text.**

My text

On Saturday I often go shopping with my dad. We go to a supermarket in Regent Street. There we buy milk, yoghurt, orange juice, bread and many other things. We also go to a farmer's market. There we buy apples, pears, potatoes, broccoli, tomatoes, carrots, eggs and cheese. One farmer also sells fish. Dad and I like fish. Dad also buys flowers for Mum.

What do you buy?

15 Do interviews in class. Make notes.

bread

orange juice

a hot dog

milk

fruit

vegetables

sweets

books

toys

CDs

chocolate

magazines

Do you often go shopping?

What do you buy?

Do you go with your mum?

How old is she?

Yes, I do.

I often buy …
I sometimes buy …
I never buy …

No, with my sister.

Fourteen.

16 Write a report. Then say.

Sarah often goes shopping. She often buys …
She sometimes buys … She never buys …
She goes shopping with her sister. Her sister is fourteen.

2 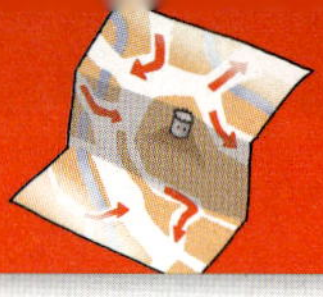 In town

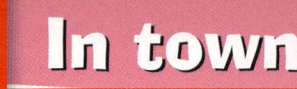

☆ **1 Work in pairs. How many words and phrases can you remember? Take notes.**

travelling
go by bus
walk
?
?
?
?
?
?

We can remember … words and phrases.

☆ **2** 1 13 **Listen and point. In pairs, point and say.**

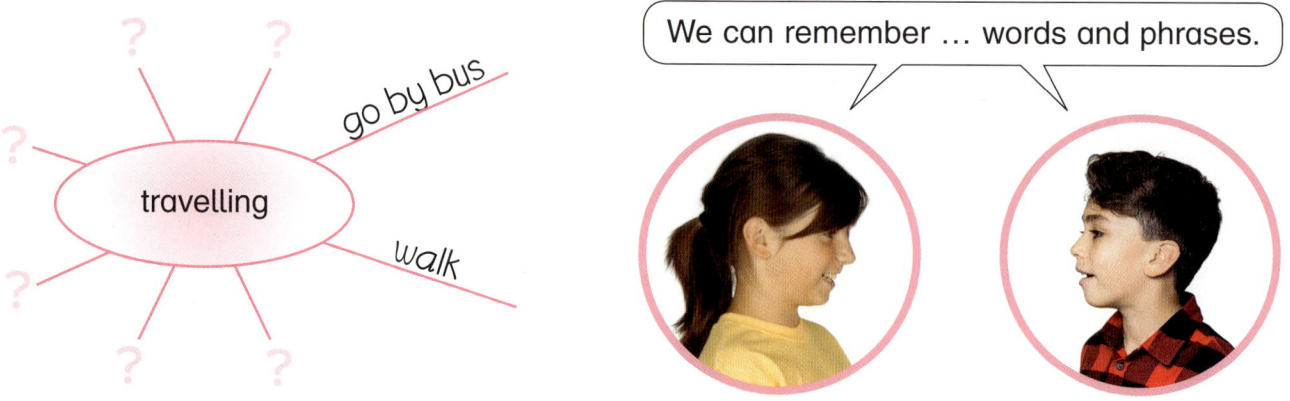

1 **restaurant**
2 **hospital**
3 **museum**
4 **zoo**
5 **swimming pool**
6 **cinema**
7 **supermarket**
8 **library**
9 **post office**
10 **sweet shop**
11 **train station**
12 **bus stop**
13 **playground**

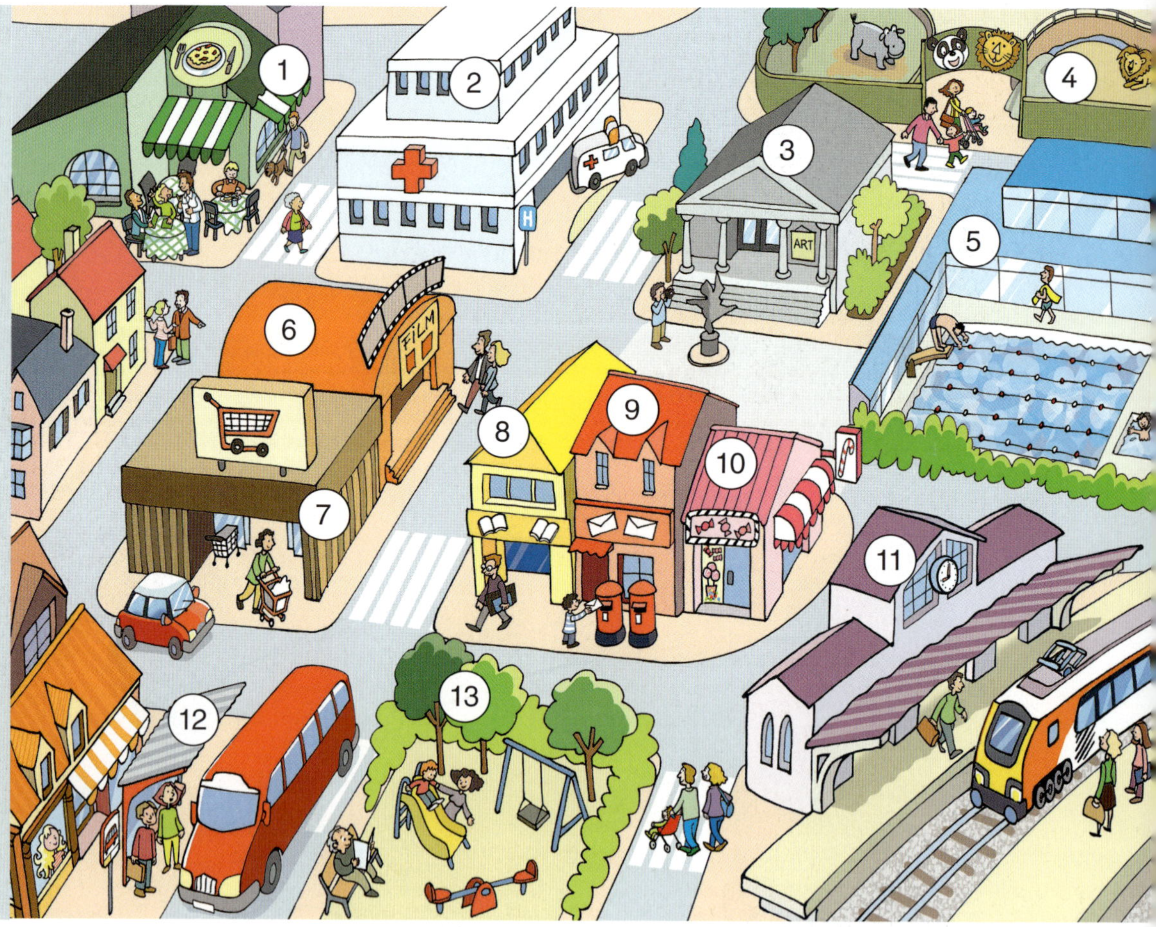
1
2
3
4
5
6
7
8
9
10
11
12
13
ART
FILM

☆☆ **3 Play the memory game.**

What's number 5?
I think it's the swimming pool.
Yes.

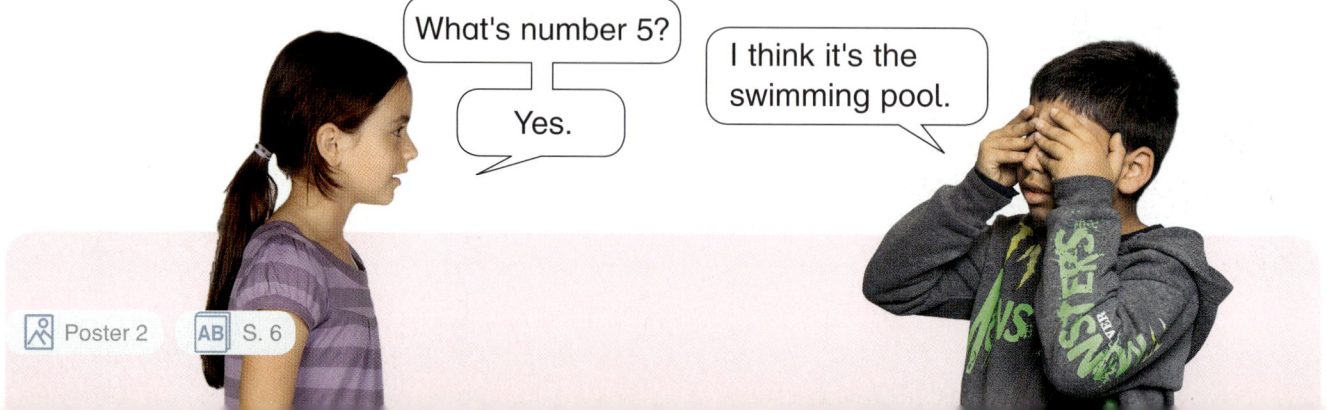

★ **4** 15 **Listen and point.**

Turn left.

Go straight on.

Turn right.

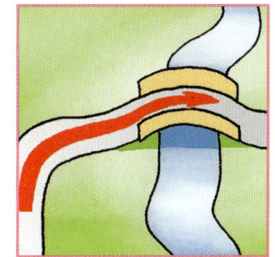

Go across the bridge.

★ **5** 16 **Listen. Then act out the dialogues.**

Dialogue 1:

Tourist: Excuse me, please. Where's the cinema?
Woman: It's in Market Street.
Tourist: Where's that?
Woman: Go straight on. Then turn right at the park.
Tourist: Thank you.

Dialogue 2:

Tourist: Excuse me, where's the supermarket?
Man: OK. Turn left here. Then go across the bridge.
You can see the supermarket from the bridge.
Tourist: Thank you very much.
Man: That's OK.

Dialogue 3:

Tourist: Excuse me, please.
Woman: Yes?
Tourist: Where's the zoo?
Woman: Look, there's a bus stop over there.
Tourist: A bus stop?
Woman: Yes, bus 18 takes you to the zoo.
Tourist: Thank you.

⭐ **6** **Look and read. Say which sentences are *True* or *False*.**

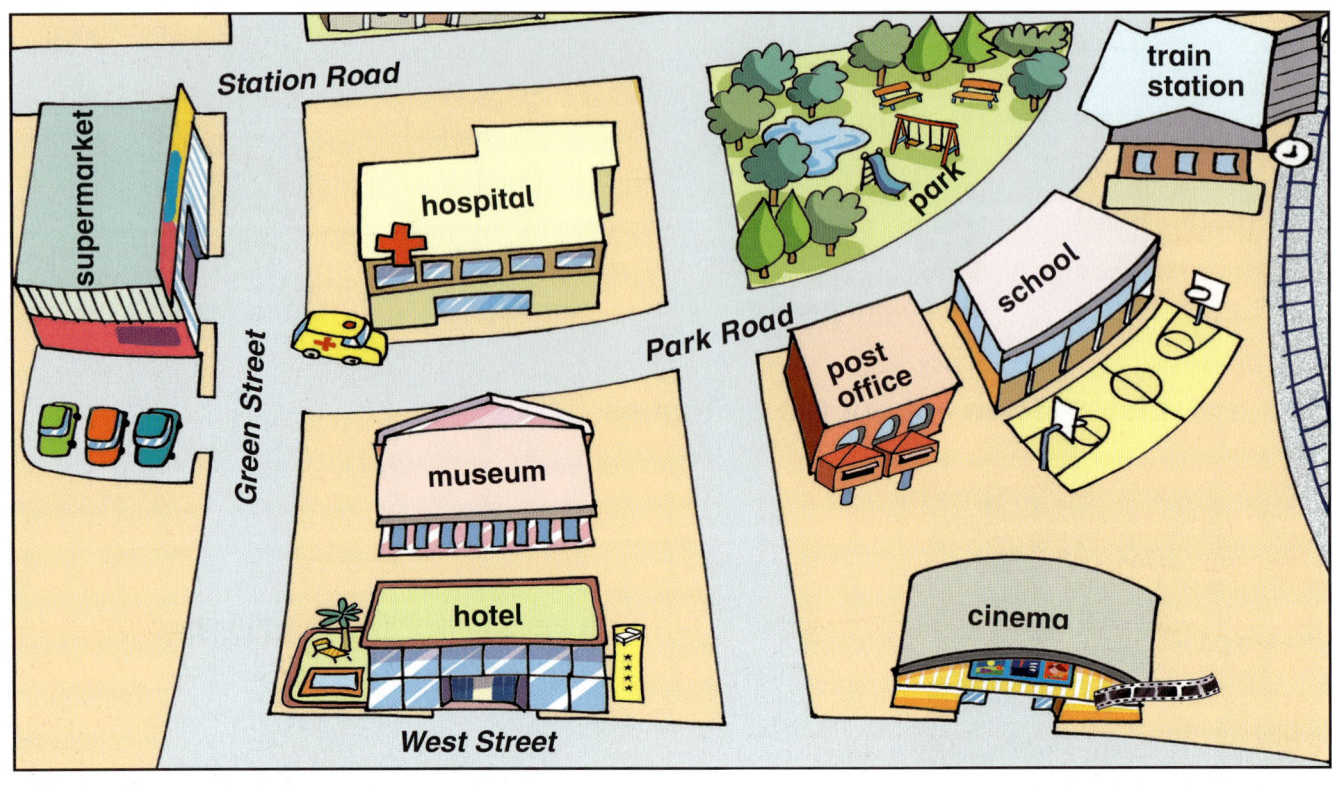

1. The post office is in Green Street.
2. The school is next to the post office.
3. The hospital is opposite the museum.
4. The school is opposite the park.
5. The cinema is next to the hospital.
6. The supermarket is in Green Street.
7. The train station is opposite the museum.
8. The hotel is in Park Road.
9. The supermarket is opposite the school.
10. The hospital is in Park Road.

L👀K!

next to   opposite

Number 1 is false.

⭐ **7** **Correct the wrong sentences from 6.**

The post office is in Park Road.

...

★ 8 🔵 18–20 **Listen. Do the chant.**

Excuse me, sir,
can you help me?
Where's the park?

Across the bridge,
then straight on,
you walk a mile or two.
Then you can see the park.
It's opposite the zoo.

Across the bridge,
then straight on,
I walk a mile or two.
Then I can see the park.
It's opposite the zoo.

That's true.

9 **Work in pairs. Speak.**

restaurant

hospital

cinema

school

post office

super-market

BUS STOP

library

playground

park

Excuse me, please.
Where's the hospital?

Go …

KV 5   AB   S. 9   **11**

10 **Read and think. Say the places.**

1 This is a place where you go to find good books. **?**

2 You go there to see lots of animals. **?**

3 This is a place where you can see lots of old things. **?**

4 You can buy chocolates, biscuits and chewing gum there. **?**

5 People go shopping for food and other things there. **?**

6 This is a place where there are lots of doctors. **?**

7 People go there to watch films. **?**

8 This is a place where people go to have lunch and dinner. **?**

9 It's a good place to go when it's very hot in the summer. **?**

10 It's a place where you can play football, and keep fit. **?**

11 **Read. Write your own text.**

My text

My house is in King's Street. It's opposite
the playground, next to the supermarket.
My favourite place in our town is the park.

12 **Read. Write your own text.**

My text

This is how you can get to my house from the school. Turn right at the bus stop
and go straight on. Then turn left at the library. Go straight on, across the bridge.
My house is on the left. It's Number 10, Green Street.
My favourite place in our town is the zoo. I often go there at weekends.

Mia and Mike in London

⭐ **13** **Look at the photos. Guess the answers.** 📺 **Then watch and check.**

1

 2

Which picture shows …
- Big Ben?
- the London Eye?
- Tower Bridge?
- Buckingham Palace?

3

 4

Number 1 is …

⭐⭐

A group project: Sightseeing in London

Practise role plays in groups.

Look over there! That's …	Wow. It looks great / very nice.
Do you know what that is?	Yes, I think it's … / I have no idea.
Let's go and see …	Yes, good idea. / No, let's go …
Let's take the bus.	No, let's walk / go by …

★ 1 🔊 21 **Listen and point. In pairs, point and say.**

1 sad
2 relaxed
3 excited
4 angry
5 nervous
6 happy
7 scared
8 tired
9 bored

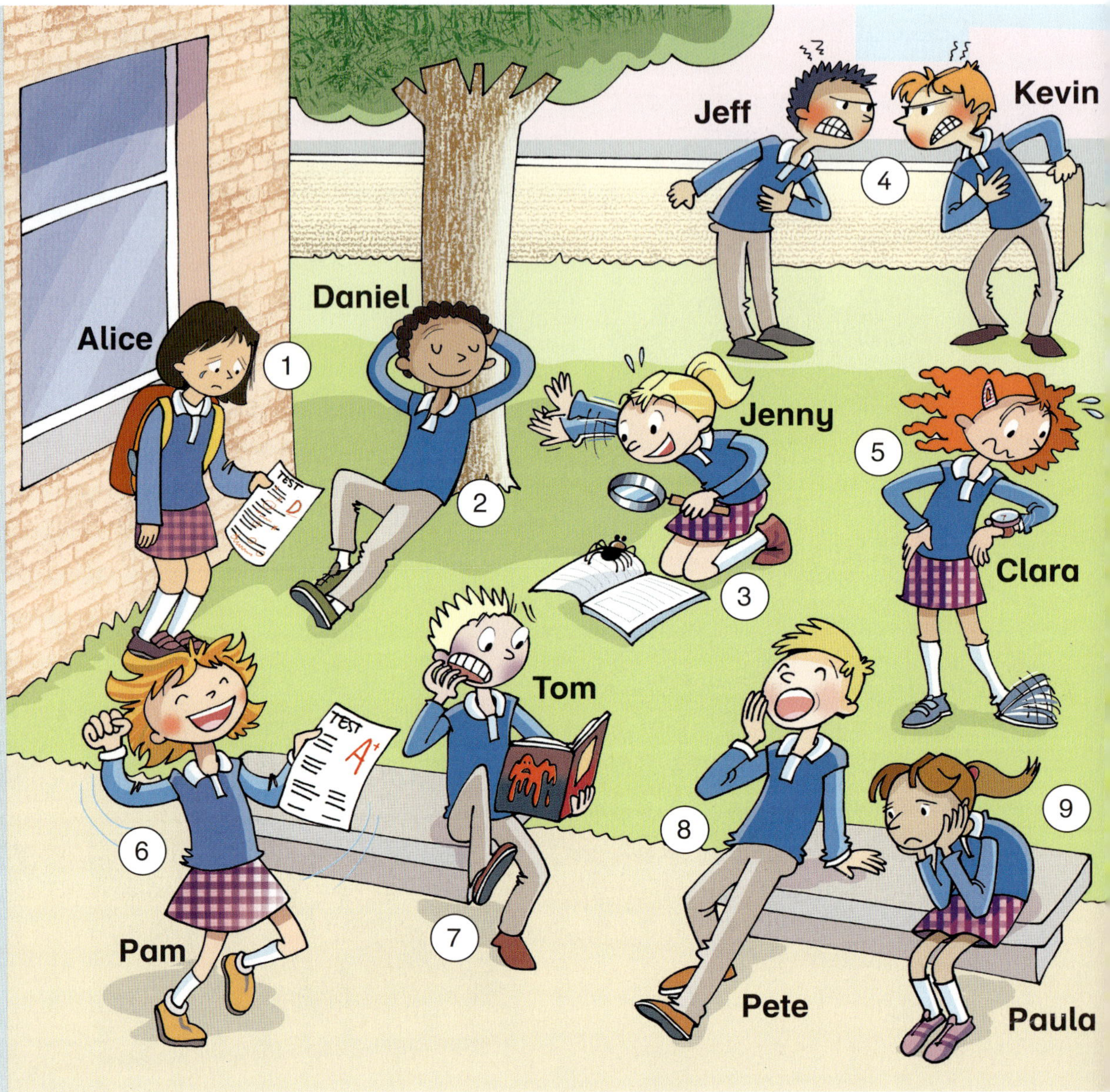

Jeff   Kevin

Daniel

Alice

Jenny

Clara

Tom

Pam

Pete   Paula

★ 2 Play the memory game.

Tell me about Jeff and Kevin.

That's right.

I think they're angry.

Tell me about Clara.

No, sorry. She's nervous.

I think she's bored.

★ **3** 24–26 **Listen. Do the chant.**

Are you happy?

Are you happy?
No, I'm not.

Are you sad?
No, I'm not.

Are you angry?
No, I'm not.

Are you tired?
No, I'm not.

What's the matter?
I'm hot.

★ **4** 27 **Listen to the dialogues.**

LOO**K!**
They're = They are
They aren't = They are not
He/She/It isn't = … is not

Dialogue 1:

Nicole: Is he bored?

Charlie: No, he isn't.

Nicole: Is he sad?

Charlie: Yes, he is.

Nicole: What's the matter?

Charlie: His dog is ill.

Dialogue 2:

Larry: Are they angry?

Susan: No, they aren't.

Larry: What's the problem?

Susan: They're hungry.

★★ **5** **Work in pairs. Change the dialogues and act them out.**

Snow White

⭐ **6** **Watch the story.** 28 **Listen and read.**

Here you are, Snow White.

Thank you, Ted.

Mirror, mirror, who's the best singer?

That's Snow White, my Queen.

The queen is very angry.

You stupid mirror!

Ted, Ted, come here!

Yes, my Queen.

Ted, kill Snow White and bring me her heart.

Where are we going, Ted?

To the airport, Snow White. You must go away.

Bye, bye, Snow White!

Ted is sad.

A sheep's heart, please.

Here you are. Two pounds, please.

Here's Snow White's heart.

Thank you, Ted.

The queen is very happy.

Snow White is in New York. She's sad.

I'm alone, I'm alone in the city ...

I love your song.

Thank you.

I'm not alone, not alone in the city ... I'm so happy ...

Snow White, you're the best singer in the world.

Soon Snow White is a big star. Millions see her on TV. The queen sees her too.

It's Snow White! She's in New York.

This is Snow White! She's the best singer in the world!

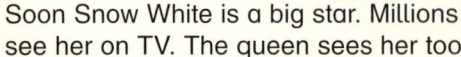

The queen is very angry.

The next day the queen flies to New York.

I'm scared. The queen is in New York. You must help Snow White!

OK.

★ **7** 29–30 **Listen. Sing the song.**

Friends

I'm not alone, not alone in the city.
I'm so happy, so happy
I've got friends.

We laugh and shout,
we run around and hop.
We sing and dance,
we never, never stop.

I'm not alone, not alone in the city.
I'm so happy, so happy
I've got friends.

⭐ **8** **Read, think and take notes.**

Write down the name of a …

… song that makes you happy.

… song that makes you sad.

… song that makes you relaxed.

… singer that makes you bored.

… band that makes you excited.

🌟 **9** **Say.**

> A song that makes me … is … .

> A band that makes me … is … .

> A singer that makes me … is … .

🌟 **10** **Read. Write your own text.**

My text

I love music. My favourite singer is Jane Silver.

She's 19 years old. She's a very good singer.

My favourite song by Jane Silver is 'Smile'.

This song makes me relaxed.

🌟 **11** **Read. Write your own text.**

My text

I haven't got a favourite singer, but I've got a favourite band. Their name is The Hot Potatoes. That's a funny name. There are four people in the band: Mick, Ringo, Kate and Milly. I really like their song 'Sunshine on a Sunday morning'. It's so cool. This song makes me really happy. My brother's favourite band is XX5. I don't like their music. It's heavy metal.

⭐12 🎵 31 Listen and point. Ask your friends.

a bee in my room	a snake in our garden	reading a book
a noisy street	a rainy day	a good football match
a beautiful picture	lots of people	a big dog in the street
singing songs	a good book	good food
a grumpy person	a birthday party	an interesting film
playing with my friends	lots of cars	school holidays

What's … in German?

No idea.

I think it's … .

⭐13 🎵 32 Listen and read the poem.

Feelings

What makes you scared? A spider under my bed.
What makes you nervous? A Maths test on a Monday morning.
What makes you relaxed? A great song.
What makes you bored? A love film on TV.
What makes you excited? A thrilling book.
What makes you happy? Playing with my cat.

⭐14 Write your own poem.

4 Weather

★ **1** Work in pairs. How many words and phrases can you remember? Take notes.

weather — cloudy — It's windy.

We can remember … words and phrases.

★ **2** 🔘 1 Listen and point. In pairs, point and say.

1 sky
2 rainbow
3 lightning
4 thunderstorm
5 dry
6 hurricane
7 wet

WARNING!

★ **3** Play the memory game.

What's number 4?

No, that's not right. Try again.

I think it's *lightning.*

Poster 4   AB S. 16

✦ 4 Read. Answer the questions.

- Which photo shows a hurricane?
- Which photo shows a rainbow?
- Which photo shows a farm?

Hi, I'm Amy and I live in Florida.
The weather here's fantastic. There's one problem: sometimes we get hurricanes. Hurricanes are very strong winds. When there's a hurricane there's no school. Can you find my photo?

Hi, I'm John.
I live in Ireland. It rains a lot here. It rains in winter, in spring, in summer and in autumn. It's always green here. When the grass is wet it's fun to play football. Can you find my photo?

Hello, I'm Judy.
I live on a farm in Australia. In summer it's very hot. Then the grass is brown and very dry. Sometimes it rains in winter. Can you find my photo?

Hello, I'm Mike and I live in Canada.
There's a lot of snow in winter and it's very cold. I like the winter. I often play outside with my friends. Can you find my photo?

✦ 5 Work in pairs and say *True* or *False*.

1. It never rains in Ireland.
2. John is from Australia.
3. Amy is from Florida.
4. There's a lot of snow in Australia.
5. Judy lives on a farm.
6. It rains a lot in Florida.

Autumn holidays

★ 7 6–7 **Listen. Sing the song.**

Crazy weather

On Monday, it's cloudy,
on Tuesday, there's rain.
On Wednesday, there's sun,
and on Thursday, rain again!

Oh, yeah, the weather's crazy,
it's crazy, yeah, that's true!
Sun, rain, fog or snow?
You never, never know!

On Friday, it's foggy,
it's cloudy and cold;
but on Saturday and Sunday,
there's sun – it looks like gold!

★ 8 **Play the guessing game.**

Class survey

Weather and seasons

 9 Make a weather chart on a piece of paper. Make notes.

	MONDAY	TUESDAY	WEDNESDAY	THURSDAY	FRIDAY	SATURDAY	SUNDAY
MORNING	SUNNY	FOGGY	RAINING	SUNNY	RAINING		
AFTERNOON	CLOUDY	CLOUDY	CLOUDY				

A week later: Ask your partner.

What was your favourite day last week?
What was the weather like?

My favourite day was Thursday.
It was sunny.

 10 Make a grid. In groups, ask and answer questions. Make notes.

What's your favourite season?

spring	summer	autumn	winter
Emma Sophie	Leo Paul Zoe		Philip

 11 Write a group report. Then talk about your group.

In our group, two children like spring.
Three children like ...

★ **1** Work in pairs. How many words and phrases can you remember? Take notes.

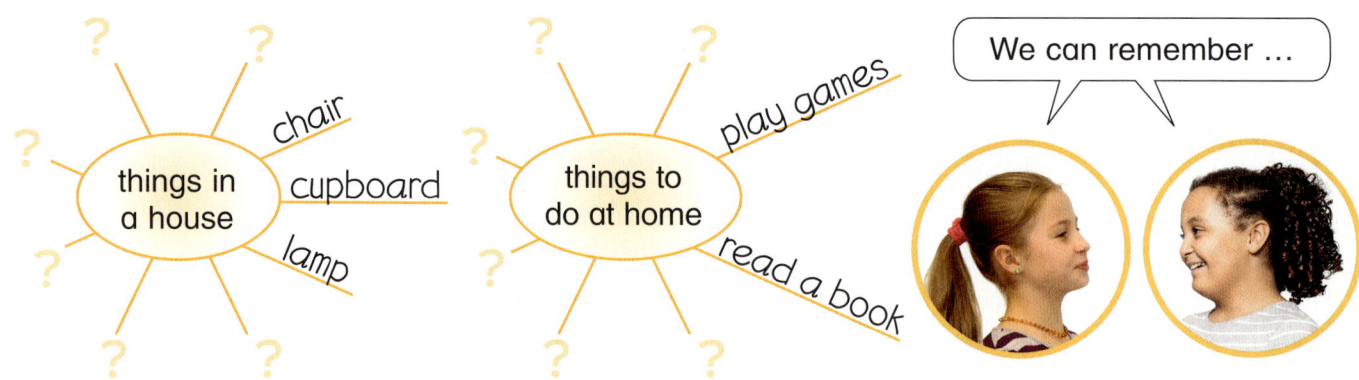

things in a house — chair, cupboard, lamp

things to do at home — play games, read a book

We can remember …

★ **2** 〈2〉 8 Listen and point. In pairs, point and say.

1 attic
2 wardrobe
3 floor
4 bed
5 bathroom
6 washbasin
7 stairs
8 bedroom
9 kitchen
10 hall
11 living room

✦ **3** Play the game. You need a coin ⬤. Ask and answer.

Where's the coin?

No, it isn't.

Is it in the kitchen?

★ **4** 🔊 10 **Listen and point. Then test your partner.**

under   next to   in

on   in front of   behind

⭐ **5** **Play the game. Ask and answer.**

Is the pencil **in** the pencil case?

Is it … ?

No, it isn't.

⭐ **6** **Look at the picture in 2. Ask and answer.**

Where are Tom's socks?	Where are Kate's trainers?
Where's his cap?	Where's her T-shirt?
Where are his jeans?	Where's her pullover?
Where's his schoolbag?	Where's her umbrella?

Where are Tom's socks?

Where are Kate's trainers?

On the sofa in the living room.

Under the … in the …

🕐 KV 13   AB S. 23   27

Rocky and Rusty

⭐ **7** 📺 **Watch the story.** 💿 11 **Listen and read.**

★ 8   12–13 Listen. Sing the song.

The raccoon in my room

There's a raccoon,
a little raccoon,
a little raccoon
in my room, oh, yes!

He's drinking my milk
and he's eating my bread,
he's breaking my toys
and he's using my bed.

Please, Mum, don't come in.
There's a mess in my room.
I think my raccoon
won't leave before June.

Don't tell anybody
my little raccoon
is just an excuse
for the mess in my room.

✦✦ 9   14 Listen and read. Answer the questions.

Unusual homes

Hi, my name is Odval, and I live in Mongolia. We live in a yurt. It's a big tent made of wood and cloth. There are five people in my family: my mum, my dad, my grandma, my brother and me. The yurt is one big room with a fireplace in the middle. There's a hole in the roof for the smoke to go out. We sleep, cook and eat in our yurt. In winter it's very warm and in summer it's nice and cool.

1 What's the girl's name?

2 Where's she from?

3 Where does she live?

4 How many people are in her family?

5 What's a yurt?

★ 10 Look, read and say.

- Emma's socks are next to the lamp.
- Ruby's socks are on the lamp.
- Molly's socks are behind the lamp.
- Matilda's socks are under the lamp.

> Emma's socks are in picture …

My text ✏

⭐ 11 Read. Write your own text.

My text

In my room, there's a nice bed.
The desk is in front of the window.
There are three posters in my room.

⭐ 12 Read. Write your own text.

My text

In our apartment there are five rooms: the bathroom, the kitchen, the living room, Mum and Dad's bedroom and the bedroom for my sister and me. In our room there are two beds, one wardrobe, two small desks and two chairs. There are lots of posters in our room. On the posters there are horses and cats. My sister loves horses and I love cats. We do our homework in our room and we play and read there. In the evening we sometimes watch TV in the living room.

Houses and homes

 13 Look at the photos and answer the questions.

Which photo shows …
- a semi-detached house?
- a house in the countryside?
- a block of flats?

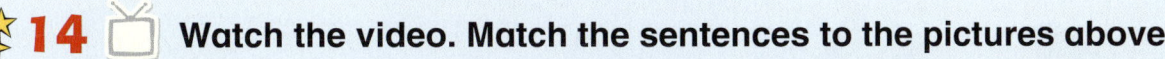 **14** 📺 **Watch the video. Match the sentences to the pictures above.**

- There are lots of cars and it's very noisy here.
- There are lots of shops, cinemas and restaurants nearby.
- It's very quiet here.
- Lots of tourists come here because it's so beautiful.
- It's two houses in one, and they look exactly the same.
- There's a bus stop and a train station near here.
- There are lots of gardens with beautiful flowers.

'It's very quiet here.' is picture number 3.

A poster project: Crazy houses

Bring pictures of crazy houses. Make a poster.

- This is my crazy house.
- It's a … house.
- It's big/small/…
- It's cool/great.

Presentation tips:
✔ Loud and clear!
✔ Smile.
✔ Point at your picture/photo.

6 At the restaurant

⭐ **1 Work in pairs. How many words can you remember? Take notes.**

tea

food and drink

peas

We can remember … words.

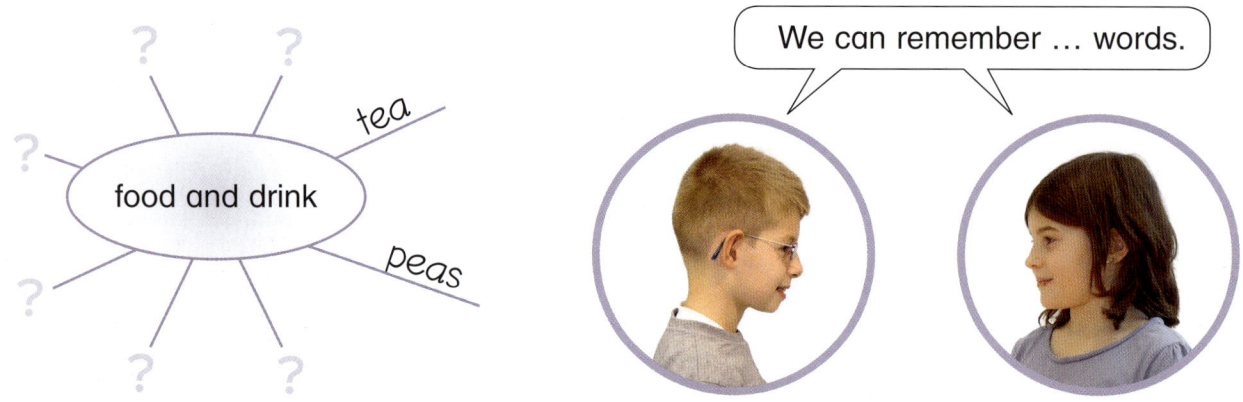

⭐ **2** 🔵2 16 **Listen and point. In pairs, point and say.**

1. steak
2. lemonade
3. mixed salad
4. pie
5. nuts
6. beans
7. sausages
8. coffee
9. fruit salad

DESSERT

Coffee £1.85

*Fruit salad £2.00

*Apple pie £2.25

⭐ **3 Ask your partner.**

Do you like … ?

Yes, I do. /
No, I don't.

Poster 6 AB S. 26 ⏱ KV 16

  4 18–19 **Listen. Sing the song.**

Luba's restaurant

Luba's is a crazy restaurant,
Luba's is the place to go.
Luba's is the place for you and me,
come here and you will see!

There is fish in your orange juice
and ice cream on your steak.
There's fruit on your pizza
and salad on your cake!

Luba's is a crazy restaurant,
Luba's is the place to go.
Luba's is the place for you and me,
come here and you will see!

There are nuts in your tomato soup
and coffee on your pie –
and on top of your dessert
there is a fly!
Oh, no!

5 Read and say *True* or *False*. Correct the wrong sentences.

1 In Luba's restaurant, there's fruit on your cake.

2 There are nuts in your tomato soup.

3 There's salad on your dessert.

4 There's fish in your orange juice.

5 There's chocolate on your steak.

6 There's coffee on your pie.

> In Luba's restaurant, there's fruit on your cake.

> That's false. In Luba's restaurant, there's fruit on your … .

 6 Create a menu for a crazy restaurant.

Toffees for Annabel

★ **7** 📺 **Watch the story.** 💿 22 **Listen and read.**

Dad, I'm hungry.

Would you like some cheese, Annabel?

Cheese? No, thanks.

What about chicken with rice and peas?

No, thanks, Dad.

I can make you some sausages with beans.

No. Please make me some toffees.

OK.

I'm so hungry, Dad.

Just a minute.

Here you are, Annabel. Don't eat too many.

Thanks, Dad. I love toffees.

Daaaad!

What is it?

I can't open my mouth.

Annabel's dad is trying to open her mouth.

Sorry, I can't help you.

Annabel's father goes to ask their neighbour for help.

Annabel can't open her mouth. Can you help me, please?

Yes, of course.

Pull! Pull!

You must call Dr Simpson.

Annabel can't open her mouth. Can you help me, please?

Soon the doctor arrives.

Sorry, Annabel. I can't help you.

Mr Brown, you must call the fire brigade.

Soon the fire brigade arrives.

Turn the water on!

8 Read the menu. Then test your partner.

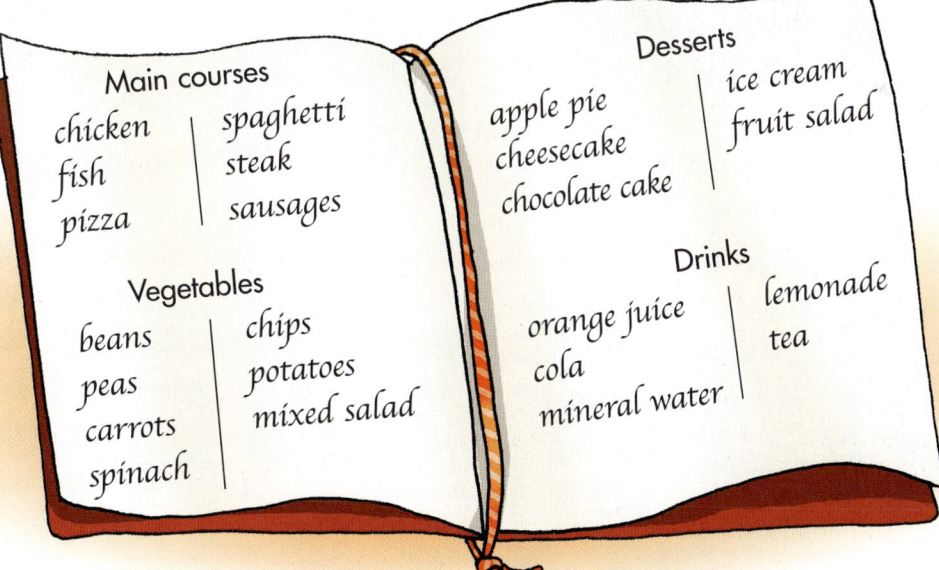

Desserts: ice cream, chocolate cake, fruit salad.

Two are missing.

⭐ **9** 🔁 23 **Listen and read.**

What would you like to eat?

Sausages and beans for me, please.

Fish and chips and a mixed salad, please.

Fish and chips and a mixed salad. And sausages and beans. And to drink?

I'm thirsty. A big cola, please.

An orange juice for me.

Here you are.

Thanks.

Pass me the salt, please.

Here you are.

Thank you.

Let's have dessert.

I want to have an ice cream, please.

I'd like a fruit salad, please.

I'd like an ice cream, please.

⭐ **10** **Do a role play.**

All that food is just for me

⭐ **11** 🔘 24 **Listen and read the poem.**

Tomato soup,
a muesli bar,
a yoghurt, apples,
chicken, tea.
All that food
is just for me.

Steak and rice,
eggs and cheese,
a cake, an orange,
can't you see?
All that food
is just for me.

How can I put
all that food
in my lunch box
for a start?
Who can help me?
Who's so smart?

⭐⭐ **12** **Write your own poem.**

mixed salad	pie	chocolate	peas	sausages
beans	ice cream	nuts	fish	pizza
chips	spaghetti	spinach	carrots	fruit salad

⭐ **1** Work in pairs. How many words can you remember? Take notes.

outdoor places — farm — forest

We can remember … words.

⭐⭐ **2** 🎧 1 Listen and point. In pairs, point and say.

1. mountain
2. beach
3. sea
4. village
5. hill
6. lake
7. road
8. field
9. river
10. motorway

⭐ **3** Play the *Read my lips* game.

I think it's motorway.

⭐ **4** 🎧 3 **Listen and find out where the treasure is.**

1					
2					
3					
4					

⭐ **5** **Work in pairs. Hide the treasure.**

Is it on green three?

Is it on blue four?

No, it isn't.

Yes, it is.

A treasure hunt

⭐ **6** 📺 Watch the story and say words you remember. Finish the sentences.

1

All right, … We're …

Help! I'm … !
You've got …

2

Oh, no. It's too …
It's too …

3

I've got it. I've got it.

…, Dad.

I …

4

But we …
Happy … , … !

I don't …

⭐ **7** 5 **Listen and read.**

Damian: Your birthday present is in a box.

Lola: OK. And where's the box?

Damian: OK, listen carefully. Go through the forest, across the field and up the hill.
The box with the treasure is in a castle.

Lola: Ah, here it is!

Damian: Open it and see what's in it.

Lola: Oh, it's chocolate. Let's share it.

Damian: Great, thanks. Happy birthday, Lola!

Lola: Thank you.

⭐ **8** Do a role play.

9   8 **Listen to the dialogue. Change it with a partner. Act it out.**

Oliver: Look, there's an old box!
Alice: Wow! Let's open it.
Oliver: Maybe there's gold in it.
Alice: Help me open it.
Oliver: OK.
Alice: I don't believe it.
Oliver: What's in it?
Alice: An old shoe!

10 Create a story and act it out. Work with a partner.

Look, there's a castle.

Finding gold – a true story

It's the year 1715.

Twelve big Spanish ships are on their way from South America to Spain. There's a lot of gold and silver on board the ships. The weather is very bad. It's raining and there's a strong wind.

Near the coast of Florida there's a hurricane. The situation is very, very bad.

There's no help for the people on the ships. The ships sink. All the people die.

It's the year 1950.

There's a man on the beach in Florida. His name is Kip Wagner. He is going for a walk. It's a beautiful day. The sun is shining. It's very warm.

Suddenly Kip Wagner sees something in the sand. It's a gold coin. It's beautiful. And it looks very old.

Kip Wagner has got an idea. 'The gold coin is from the year 1715. It's from the Spanish ships,' he thinks.

Kip Wagner starts looking at the sand around him. He finds more and more gold. He gets very excited and makes a plan.

Kip Wagner hires a plane and a team of people. They want to find the ship. They fly the plane over the sea. They all look very carefully.

Kip Wagner and his team are lucky. They find a big treasure, and it's from the Spanish ships – ten thousand gold coins and a hundred thousand silver coins!

Here are some of the gold coins that Kip Wagner and his team found:

What do you collect?

12 Do interviews in class. Make notes.

football pictures

animal pictures

shells

rocks

coins

stickers

cuddly toys

magazines

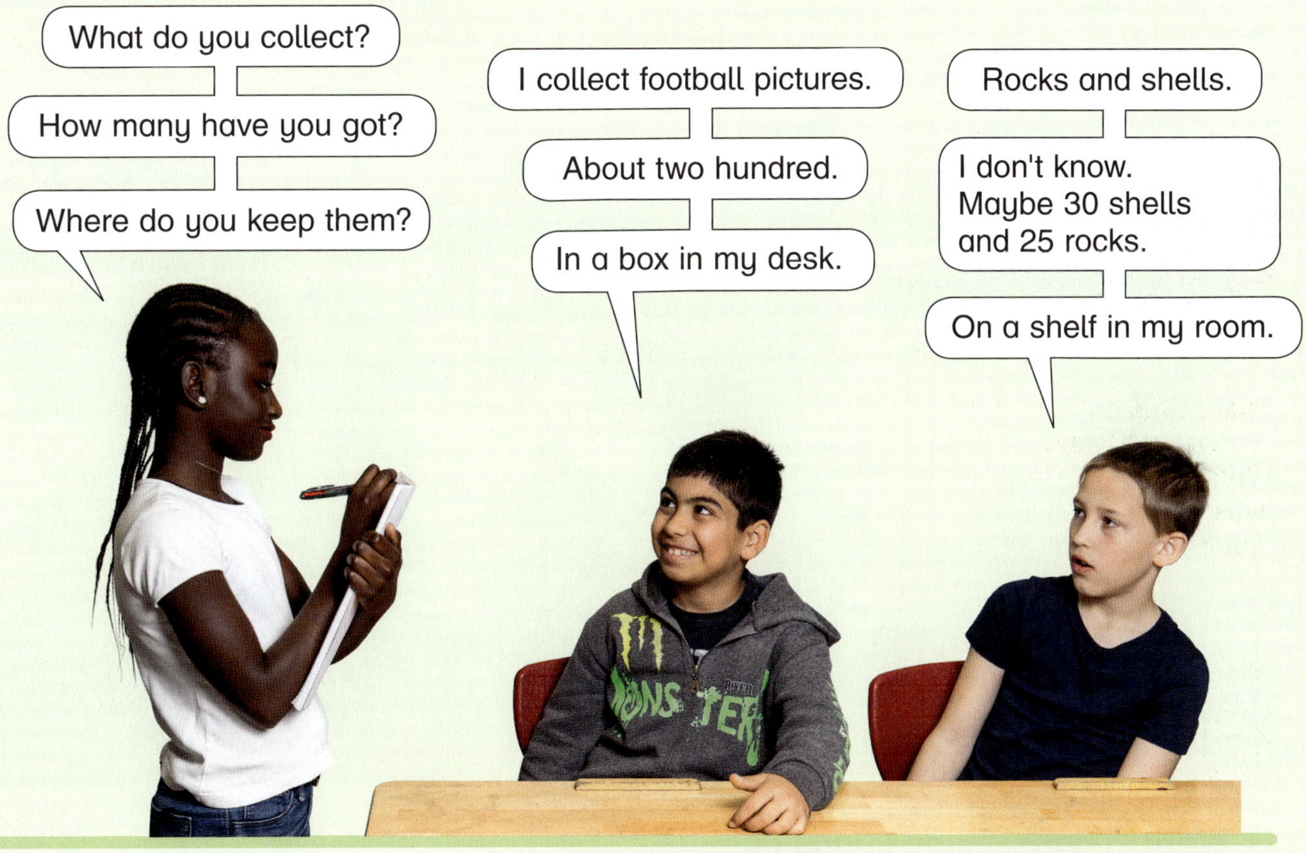

What do you collect?

How many have you got?

Where do you keep them?

I collect football pictures.

About two hundred.

In a box in my desk.

Rocks and shells.

I don't know. Maybe 30 shells and 25 rocks.

On a shelf in my room.

13 Write a group report. Then talk about your group.

Andy collects football pictures. He has got about two hundred. He keeps them in a box in his desk. Robert collects rocks and shells. He doesn't know how many he has got, but he thinks he has got thirty shells and twenty-five rocks. He keeps them on a shelf in his room.

★ **1** Work in pairs. How many words and phrases can you remember? Take notes.

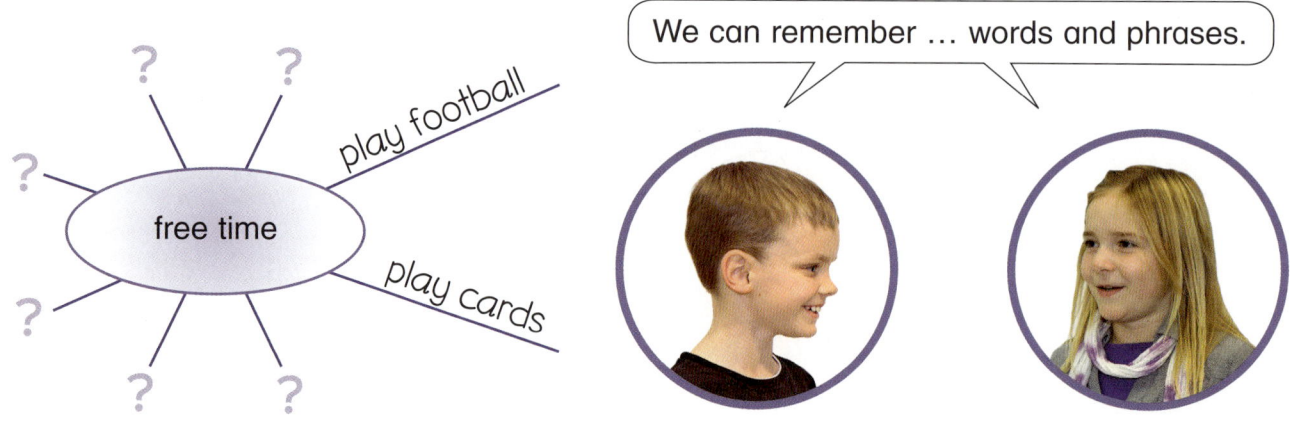

We can remember … words and phrases.

free time
? ? ? ? ? ?
play football
play cards

★ **2** 🎧 3 10 Listen and point. In pairs, point and say.

1. build a robot
2. paint a picture
3. fly a kite
4. play an instrument
5. cook
6. dance
7. feed animals
8. swim
9. snorkel
10. ride a bike
11. sail a boat
12. skate

CAMP ACTIVITIES

★ **3** Work in pairs. Mime and guess.

Swim.

Poster 8   AB S. 36

4 12–13 **Listen. Sing the song.**

Busy Lizzy

Her name is Lizzy,
and she's so busy.
She's got so many
things to do.

She feeds the squirrels in the park,
she plays the saxophone.
She rides her bike around the town
and then she dances with a clown.

Her name is ...

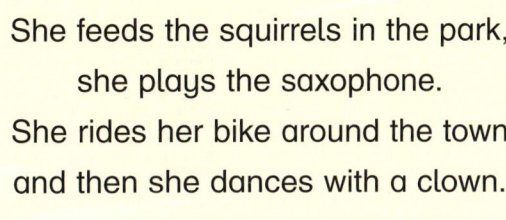

She goes sailing every day,
and she plays volleyball.
She cooks spaghetti for her friends,
her busy day just never ends.

Her name is ...

 5 **Read and find the mistakes. Say the correct sentences.**

1 Lizzy feeds the ducks in the park.

2 She plays the piano.

3 Lizzy dances with a sheriff.

4 She goes shopping every day.

5 Lizzy plays basketball.

6 She cooks fish and chips for her friends.

Lizzy feeds the … in the park.

6 🎧 15 **Listen and remember. Then talk about the children.**

Claire

Robert

Abigail

James

 **7 Ask a partner.**

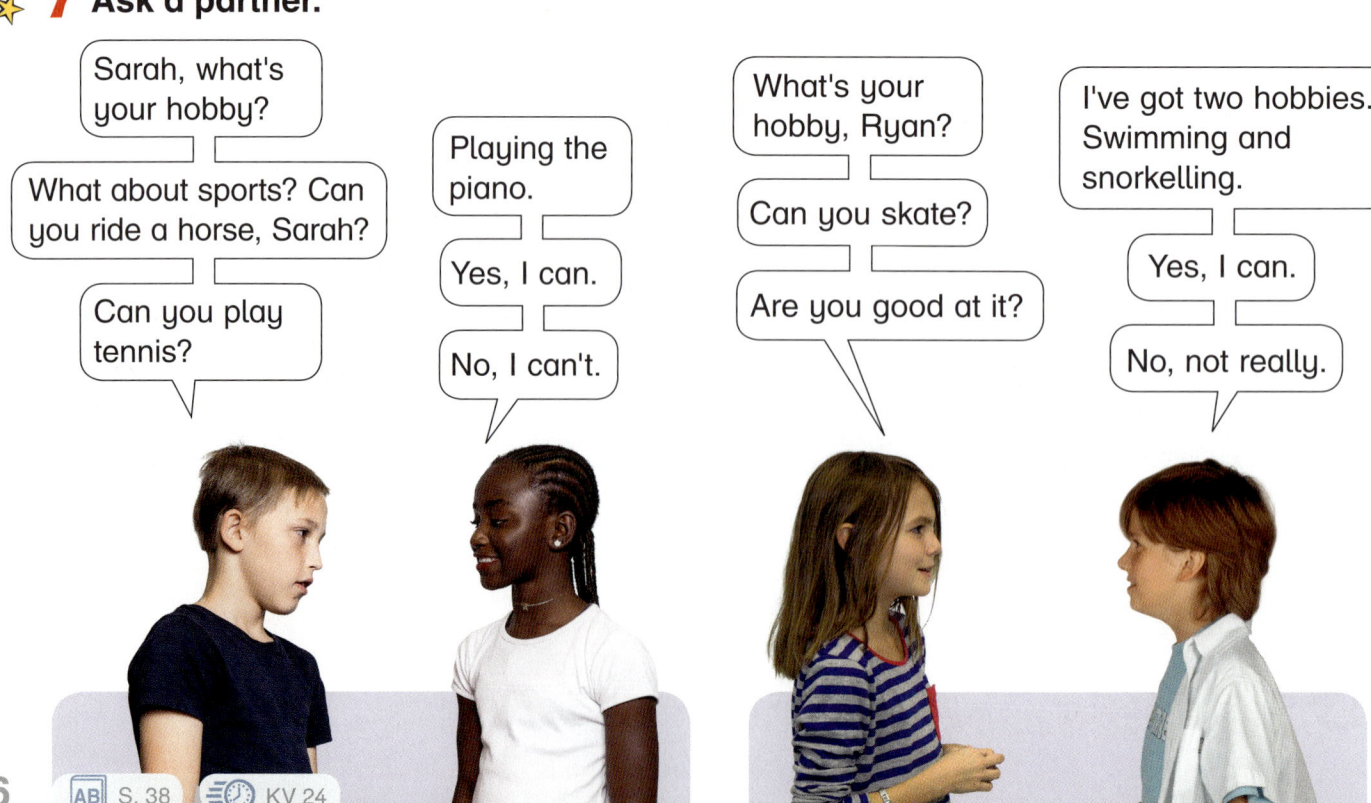

Sarah, what's your hobby?

What about sports? Can you ride a horse, Sarah?

Can you play tennis?

Playing the piano.

Yes, I can.

No, I can't.

What's your hobby, Ryan?

Can you skate?

Are you good at it?

I've got two hobbies. Swimming and snorkelling.

Yes, I can.

No, not really.

| AB | S. 38 | ⏱ KV 24

A sport for Mr Matt

 8 📺 **Watch the story and say words you remember. Finish the sentences.**

1. Oh, Dad. You …

2. I'll get you!

Tennis …

3. Can we have our ball back please, Mr Matt?

Yes. Can I … ?

4. Nice skateboard. …

Sure. Go ahead.

 9 16 **Listen and read.**

Peter: Grace, you watch too much television. You need a hobby.

Grace: I've got a hobby.

Peter: What is it?

Grace: Playing computer games.

Peter: Stop playing computer games. Do some sport.

Grace: Sport? I'm not sure.

Peter: You can try running.

Grace: Running? I don't like it.

Peter: What about tennis?

Grace: That's boring. But I've got an idea. I can try skateboarding.

Peter: That's it!

 10 Do a role play.

★ 11 🎧 ³ 17 Listen and read.

Interviewer:	Trevor, what's your hobby?
Trevor:	Let me think. OK, I've got two hobbies.
Interviewer:	Really?
Trevor:	Yes. My hobbies are cooking and playing football.
Interviewer:	Cooking? Really?
Trevor:	Yeah, I like cooking, but I'm not so good at it.
Interviewer:	What about football?
Trevor:	It's my favourite sport.

★ 12 Read and find the mistakes. Say the correct sentences.

1 Trevor has got one hobby.

2 Trevor doesn't like cooking.

3 Trevor's hobbies are cooking and swimming.

4 Trevor can't play football.

★ 13 In groups, talk about your hobby.

My text ✏️

★ 14 Read. Write your own text.

My text

Cooking is my hobby. I'm good at it.
I can play the guitar.
I can't play the piano.

★ 15 Read. Write your own text.

My text

My hobby is flying a kite. I've got three kites. In autumn I fly my kites every day.
My best friend is William. His hobby is playing football. He's very good at it. We
often play football together. William can also play tennis. I can't. My sister is 15
years old. Her hobby is swimming. She's very good at it. She's in the school team.

Hobbies

⭐ **16 Look at the photos. Talk about the children's hobbies.**

1 Bryan

2 Isabel

3 Lucy

Who likes …
- metal detecting?
- cooking?
- bird watching?

Bryan's hobby is …

⭐ **17**  **Watch the video. Who does what?**

Bryan

Isabel

Lucy

… shows Mia and Mike a cormorant.

… often cooks for his family.

… sometimes finds things on the beach.

… is making chocolate strawberries.

… has got a box full of metal things.

… loves puffins.

 A poster project: Present your hobby

Bring pictures of your hobbies. Collect English words – ask your teacher for help.

- My hobby is …
- For my hobby I need …
- Every Saturday … / I often …
- I really love my hobby. It's great fun / very interesting.

Presentation tips:
- ✔ Loud and clear!
- ✔ Smile.
- ✔ Point at your picture / photo.

⭐ **1** Work in pairs. How many words can you remember? Take notes.

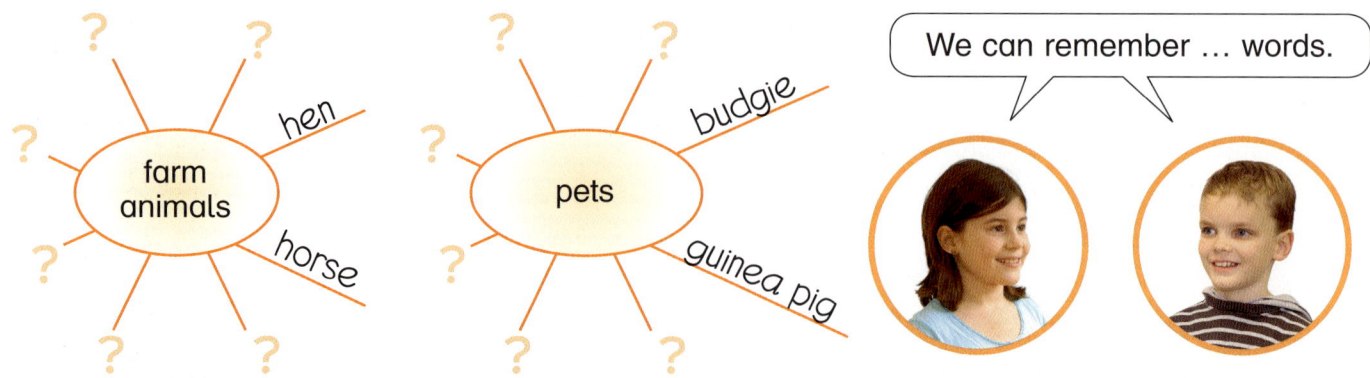

farm animals — hen, horse

pets — budgie, guinea pig

We can remember … words.

⭐ **2** 🎵 18 Listen and point. In pairs, point and say.

1 giraffe
2 polar bear
3 penguin
4 owl
5 seagull
6 leopard
7 rattlesnake
8 kangaroo
9 whale
10 seal
11 shark
12 crocodile

WELCOME TO THE SUNSHINE ZOO

⭐ **3** Play the guessing game.

What is it? Is it the crocodile?

Is it the shark?

No, it isn't.

Yes, it is.

Poster 9   AB S. 40

★ **4** 20–21 **Listen. Sing the song.**

Jungle Party

In the jungle, in the jungle
there's a party tonight.

In the jungle, in the jungle
there's a party tonight.

Arnie, the croc
is dancing on a rock.
The hippo in red socks
is swinging with the fox.

The monkey and the cat
are playing with the rat.
The lion and the frog
are singing with the dog.

The mouse and the raccoon
have got a blue balloon.
The bird and the snake
are eating all the cake.

★ **5** **Read and say.**

1 Who's eating all the cake?

2 Who's playing with the cat?

3 Who's dancing on a rock?

4 Who's swinging with the fox?

5 Who's singing with the dog?

6 Who has got a blue balloon?

… is eating all the cake.

Pinky, the elephant

★ **6** **Watch the story.** 22 **Listen and read.**

Many, many years ago, elephants had short noses. Why have they got long noses now? Here's the story.
One day, Pinky, the elephant, goes down to the river. There he meets a crocodile …

Hello, crocodile. How are you today?

Please come closer. I can't hear you.

When Pinky is very close, the crocodile grabs his nose and pulls.

Help! It hurts!

Oh, look at my nose! It hurts!

It looks funny, but it looks useful too.

A big snake hears Pinky and she comes to help him. After an hour, the crocodile lets go.

On his way home, Pinky is very hungry. He picks some fruit from a tree.

When Pinky gets home, all the elephants in his family laugh. Pinky smiles and picks some fruit from a tree.

That's great!

Wow!

Then he drinks some water with his long nose.

That's easy, Johnny!

Wonderful, Pinky. Where can I get such a long nose?

Go down to the river. Say hello to the big crocodile.

HELP! HELP!

Hee hee hee!

When Johnny comes back, all the other elephants say …

What a wonderful nose!

Let's go down to the river.

Yes, come on! Let's run.

7 Work in pairs. Look at the animals on page 50 again. Ask and answer.

Which of the animals …

… can fly?

… have got four legs?

… have got two legs?

… can climb trees?

… eat other animals?

… live in Africa?

… live in Australia?

Which of the animals can fly?

Are you sure?

Let me see. The owl, the seagull and the penguin.

Penguins can't fly.

8 Play the animal guessing game.

Has it got four legs?
Has it got two legs?
Has it got fur?
Has it got feathers?

Can it fly?
Can it climb trees?
Can it swim?

Is it big?
Is it small?
Is it a …?

Does it live in …?
Does it eat fruit?
Does it eat grass?
Does it lay eggs?
Does it eat other animals?

My text ✏️

9 Read. Write an animal riddle. Can your friends guess what it is?

My text

It's a big cat. It eats other animals. It can climb trees. Its fur is brown and black. What is it?

10 Read. Write an animal riddle. Can your friends guess what it is?

My text

My favourite animal has got four legs. It can't fly, and it can't swim. It likes cheese, but it doesn't like cats. Can you guess what it is?

⭐ **11** **Read and say *True* or *False*.**

BRISTOL ZOO GARDENS

Come to our zoo and see our fantastic animals. We are open every day from 9.00 to 5.00 (on Saturdays and Sundays too). We have 300 different kinds of animals from all over the world.

There are lions from Africa and tigers from India. Come and see our monkeys. They are fun to watch. Or visit our bird house. There are lots of colourful parrots.

We have a butterfly house too. And we have a big aquarium – there are sharks, seals and penguins.

Have you got a question about animals? Ask our zookeepers. They've got all the answers. And when you are tired or hungry, visit our café. We've got lots of delicious food.

1 There are tigers at Bristol Zoo Gardens.

2 There are two bird houses.

3 There are no sharks in the aquarium.

4 There's a special house for the butterflies.

5 There are no seals.

6 There's no café.

⭐ **12** 🎧 23 **Listen and answer.**

1 How old is the little polar bear?

2 What's her name?

3 Where's the polar bear from?

4 Where are her parents from?

5 What's her favourite food?

The little polar bear is … months old. Her name …

My zoo

⭐ 13 Read the text. Find the correct picture.

In my crazy zoo, there are a lot of fantastic animals from all over the world. We've got five elephants and eleven birds. The elephants are very small. They're red, blue and pink. The birds are lovely. They're so colourful.

> It's picture number …

✨ 14 ③ 26 Listen to the rhyme. Then practise it.

This is my super zoo.
Come and see it – it's for you.

There are fifteen elephants,
there are nineteen frogs,
there are thirteen snakes,
but there are no dogs.

There are eleven crocodiles,
there are fourteen rats,
there are twenty hippos,
but there are no cats.

✨ 15 Write your own rhyme.

Goodbye with a smile

The school party

⭐ **1** 📺 **Watch the story and say words you remember. Finish the sentences.**

1

Is she … ?

No, Dad. She's …

2

Our guitarist is ill. We can't play. I'm …

3

Danny! Daisy!

Sorry, Dad. …

4

But who's the guitarist?

I …

⭐ **2** 💿³ 27–28 **Listen. Sing the song.**

The school party

It's good to be with all your friends,
let's hope this party never ends.
It's good to sing and shout 'hooray'!
I'd like a party every day.

Let's dance, dance, dance!
Everybody let's clap, clap, clap!
Everybody let's stamp, stamp, stamp!
Everybody let's wave our hands and shout
'hooray'!

3 Read the jokes.

Laughter is the best medicine

What goes black white black white black white black white? –
A penguin rolling down a hill.

Why does a giraffe have such a long neck? –
Because its feet smell.

Why do birds fly south in winter? –
Because it's too far to walk!

What has four legs but can't walk? –
A table!

What has two hands, a round face, always runs, but doesn't move? –
A clock!

4   29 Listen and read the poem.

A friend tells me a joke.
Ha ha, ho ho, he he.
I just can't stop.
I laugh and laugh and laugh.

My tummy hurts.
And I feel good.
The world is so much fun.
Laughter is so good for me!
Ha ha, ho ho, he he.

1 🎵 30 **Listen. Say the rhymes.**

Halloween

Halloween, Halloween,
scary things can be seen,
witches' hats, coal-black cats,
ghosts and monsters, mice and rats.

Trick or treat!

Witches, ghosts and goblins
running down the street,
knock on every doorway,
'Trick or treat!'

When your door is opened,
this is what you meet,
scary creatures shouting,
'Trick or treat!'

2 🎵 31 **Listen and read.**

October 31 is Halloween.

Children in Britain and the USA dress up as witches, ghosts and monsters. There are a lot of Halloween parties. At parties, children play games like apple bobbing. To play apple bobbing, children catch an apple in a bowl of water with their mouths.

Children eat fun food and they make pumpkin lanterns. On the night of Halloween, children go from door to door. They call 'Trick or treat'. People give them sweets.

Special days

"Hi, I'm Ella from Sydney. This is our Christmas."

In Australia, Christmas is in summer, so it's sunny and hot outside.
We have our summer holidays at Christmas.
Many families celebrate Christmas on the beach.
We have a barbecue.
Here is my family on Christmas Day.

Santa Claus comes on a sleigh with six kangaroos.

AUSTRALIA 15ᶜ
CHRISTMAS 1977

"Hi, I'm Carter from Calgary."

In Canada, Christmas is in winter, so it's very cold outside. There's a lot of snow.

Here in Calgary, many families like to decorate their houses with lights. This is our house.
In the afternoon, I go on a sleigh ride with Mom and Dad.

1 33 **Listen and read.**

February 14 is Valentine's Day.
You send a card to someone
you love or like very much.
But you don't write your name.
Children make cards for their mums
and dads, their teachers and friends!
Some classes decorate their
classroom with hearts.

2 34 **Listen to the Valentine's poems. Say the poems.**

Roses are red,
violets are blue.
Happy Valentine's Day
from a friend – guess who?

Valentines, valentines
red, white and blue.
I'll make a nice one
and send it to you.

3 **Make your own Valentine cards.**

4 **Write cards to three friends.**

Special days

 1 35 **Listen and read.**

Pancake Day is 47 days before Easter.
On Pancake Day, many families make pancakes.
They eat the hot pancakes with sugar and lemon juice.
There are many pancake races.
At a pancake race, children run with a pancake in a pan.
When they are running, they toss their pancakes.

 2  36–38 **Listen. Do the chant.**

Mix a pancake

Mix a pancake,
stir a pancake,
put it in the pan.
Fry the pancake,
toss the pancake,
catch it if you can.

 3 **Make pancakes.**

Pancake Day pancakes
(for 12 small pancakes)

① 100 g flour
   pinch of salt
   2 eggs

② 300 ml milk
③ 50 ml oil

④ Fry the pancake.
   Eat with lemon juice
   and sugar.

Word list

English – German

A

across (the bridge)	**über** (die Brücke)
again	wieder
airport	Flughafen
alone	alleine
angry	wütend
animal	Tier
attic	Dachboden
autumn	Herbst
away	weg

B

bathroom	Badezimmer
beach	Strand
beans	Bohnen
beautiful	schön
bed	Bett
bedroom	Schlafzimmer
bee	Biene
behind	hinter
believe	glauben
bird	Vogel
birthday	Geburtstag
biscuit	Keks
block of flats	Wohnblock
book	Buch
bored	gelangweilt
boring	langweilig
box	Kiste
bread	Brot
bridge	Brücke
build a robot	einen Roboter bauen
burglar	Einbrecher
bus stop	Bushaltestelle
busy	(viel)beschäftigt
butterfly	Schmetterling
buy	kaufen

C

cake	Torte
call	anrufen
cap	Mütze, Kappe
Listen **carefully**.	Hör gut zu.
castle	Burg
chair	Stuhl
cheese	Käse
chewing gum	Kaugummi
chicken	Huhn
chips	Pommes frites
chocolate	Schokolade
cinema	Kino
city	Stadt
climb trees	auf Bäume klettern
cloth	Stoff
coast	Küste
coffee	Kaffee
coin	Münze
collect	sammeln
colourful	farbenfroh
cook	kochen
cormorant	Kormoran
in the **countryside**	auf dem **Land**
crazy	verrückt
create	erstellen
crocodile	Krokodil
cuddly toy	Kuscheltier

D

dad	Papa
dance	tanzen
day	Tag
desk	Schreibtisch
dessert	Nachspeise
door	Tür
down	hinunter
drink	trinken; Getränk
dry	trocken

E

eat	essen
eighty	achtzig
evening	Abend
excited	aufgeregt
Excuse me.	Entschuldige bitte. / Entschuldigen Sie bitte.

F

farm	Bauernhof
farmer's market	Bauernmarkt
favourite	Lieblings-
feather	Feder
feed animals	Tiere **füttern**
field	Feld
finish	fertigstellen
fireplace	Feuerstelle
fist	Faust
fifty	fünfzig
fire brigade	Feuerwehr
floor	Boden
flower	Blume
fly	fliegen
fly a kite	einen Drachen steigen lassen
food	Essen, Nahrungsmittel
forest	Wald
forty	vierzig
Friday	Freitag
friends	Freundinnen / Freunde
fruit salad	Fruchtsalat
funny	lustig
fur	Pelz, Fell

G

German	Deutsch
great	großartig
grumpy	mürrisch
guess	raten
guitar	Gitarre
guitarist	Gitarrist

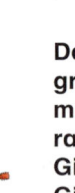

H

hall	Hausflur
happy	glücklich
heart	Herz
help	helfen
(play) **hide and seek**	Verstecken spielen
hill	Hügel
hippo	Flusspferd
hire	mieten
hobby	Freizeitbeschäftigung
hole	Loch
holidays	Ferien
homework	Hausübung
hospital	Krankenhaus

hot	heiß
How much …?	Wie viel …?
How old …?	Wie alt …?
(two) **hundred**	(zwei)**hundert**
hungry	hungrig
hurricane	Hurrikan/Wirbelsturm
hurt	wehtun

I

ice cream	Eiscreme
I'd like …	Ich hätte gerne …
ill	krank
in front of	vor
It's my turn.	Ich bin an der Reihe.

J

joke	Witz
jungle	Dschungel

K

kangaroo	Känguru
keep	hier: **aufbewahren**
keep fit	sich fit halten
kitchen	Küche
know	wissen

L

lake	See
last	letzte/r
laugh	lachen
laughter	Lachen
lemonade	Limonade
library	Bücherei
lightning	Blitz
lion	Löwe
live	leben
living room	Wohnzimmer
lots of / a lot of	viele
love	lieben
They **are lucky.**	Sie **haben Glück.**

M

magazine	Zeitschrift
main course	Hauptspeise
map	Landkarte
Maths	Mathe
maybe	vielleicht
meet	treffen
menu	Speisekarte
mess	Unordnung, Durcheinander
milk	Milch
mirror	Spiegel
missing	fehlend
mixed salad	gemischter Salat
Monday	Montag
monkey	Affe
month	Monat
motorway	Autobahn
mountain	Berg
mouth	Mund
mum	Mama
museum	Museum

N

nearby	in der Nähe
neighbour	Nachbar/in

nervous	nervös
never	nie
next to	neben
ninety	neunzig
noisy	laut
No way!	Auf keinen Fall!
number	Zahl
nuts	Nüsse

O

Of course.	Natürlich.
often	oft
old	alt
on	auf
opposite	gegenüber
orange juice	Orangensaft
outside	draußen
over there	dort drüben
owl	Eule

P

paint a picture	ein Bild malen
parrot	Papagei
peas	Erbsen
pen	Füllfeder, Kugelschreiber
pencil	Bleistift
pencil case	Federmappe
penguin	Pinguin
people	Leute, Menschen
piano	Klavier
pick	pflücken
picture	Bild
pie	Kuchen, Pastete
piggy bank	Sparschwein
pillow fight	Kissenschlacht
place	Ort
play an instrument	ein Instrument spielen
playground	Spielplatz
polar bear	Eisbär
post office	Postamt
pound	**Pfund** (engl. Währung)
practise	üben
pull a face	eine Grimasse schneiden
puffin	Papageientaucher

Q

queen	Königin
quiet	ruhig

R

raccoon	Waschbär
rainbow	Regenbogen
rainy	regnerisch
rattlesnake	Klapperschlange
raven	Rabe
read	lesen
I'm **ready.**	Ich bin **bereit.**
relaxed	entspannt
remember	erinnern
ride a bike	Fahrrad fahren
river	Fluss
road	Straße
rock	Fels, Stein
roof	Dach
room	Zimmer

rubber	Radiergummi
run	laufen, rennen

S

sad	traurig
salt	Salz
sail (a boat)	segeln
Saturday	Samstag
sausages	Würstchen
scared	ängstlich, verängstigt
scissors	Schere
sea	Meer
seagull	Möwe
seal	Robbe
see	sehen
seventy	siebzig
share	teilen
shark	Hai
sheep	Schaf
shell	Muschel
(go) **shopping**	einkaufen (gehen)
shopping list	Einkaufsliste
short	kurz
shout	rufen
show	zeigen
sightseeing	Sehenswürdigkeiten besichtigen
silver	Silber
sister	Schwester
sixty	sechzig
skate	skaten
smoke	Rauch
snorkel	schnorcheln
snow	Schnee
sky	Himmel
socks	Socken
something	etwas
sometimes	manchmal
South America	Südamerika
Spain	Spanien
spider	Spinne
spinach	Spinat
spring	Frühling
squirrel	Eichhörnchen
stairs	Treppe
steal	stehlen
straight on	geradeaus
strawberry	Erdbeere
street	Straße
strong	stark
stupid	dumm
suddenly	plötzlich
summer	Sommer
Sunday	Sonntag
sweet shop	Süßigkeitenladen
sweets	Süßigkeiten
swim	schwimmen
swimming pool	Schwimmbad

T

I'll **take** it.	Ich **nehme** es.
take notes	Notizen machen
tea	Tee
tell	erzählen, sagen
ten	zehn
tent	Zelt

That's all.	Das ist alles.
their	ihr/e
things	Dinge
thirsty	durstig
thirty	dreißig
thousand	tausend
thrilling	spannend, packend
through	durch
thunderstorm	Gewitter
Thursday	Donnerstag
tickle	kitzeln
tired	müde
toffee	Karamellbonbon
tonight	heute Abend
too	auch
too much	zu viel
town	Stadt, Kleinstadt
toys	Spielsachen
tracks	Spuren
train station	Bahnhof
trainers	Turnschuhe
travelling	Reisen
treasure	Schatz
treasure hunt	Schatzsuche
true	wahr
Tuesday	Dienstag
turn right/left	nach rechts/links abbiegen
twenty	zwanzig

U

umbrella	Schirm
under	unter
understand	verstehen
use	verwenden

V

vegetables	Gemüse
very	sehr
village	Dorf
visit	besuchen

W

walk	zu Fuß gehen
want	möchten, wollen
wardrobe	Kleiderschrank
washbasin	Waschbecken
weather	Wetter
Wednesday	Mittwoch
weekend	Wochenende
wet	nass
whale	Wal
What's the matter?	Was ist los?
where	wo
window	Fenster
witch	Hexe
world	Welt

Z

zookeeper	Tierpfleger